# The Wild West in American History

# INDIANS

### Written by Leonard J. Matthews
### Illustrated by Geoff Campion and others

© 1989 Rourke Publications, Inc.

**LIBRARY OF CONGRESS**
**Library of Congress Cataloging-in-Publication Data**

Matthews, Leonard.
   Indians / by Leonard Matthews.
     p.     cm.—(The Wild West in American history)
   Summary: Traces the battles waged by various North American Indian tribes and leaders to defend their land and way of life from encroaching white settlers, soldiers, and hunters.
   ISBN 0-86625-364-5
   1. Indians of North America—Wars—Juvenile literature.
[1. Indians of North America—Wars.   2. West (U.S.)—History.]
I. Title.  II. Series.
E81.M28   1988
973—dc19                         87-30703
                                             CIP
                                              AC

Britannica Home Library Service, Inc. offers a varied selection of bookcases. For details on ordering, please write:

     Britannica Home Library Service, Inc.
     310 South Michigan Avenue
     Chicago, Illinois 60604
     Attn: Customer Service

### Rourke Publications, Inc.
### Vero Beach, Florida 32964

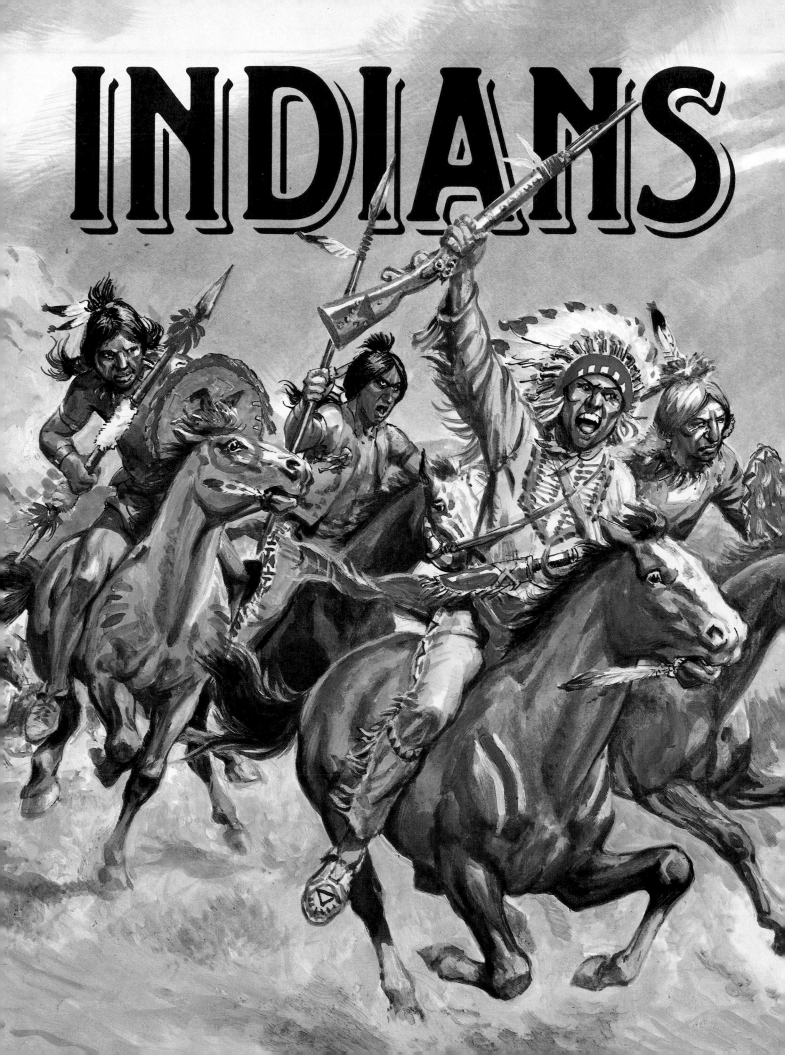

# INDIANS

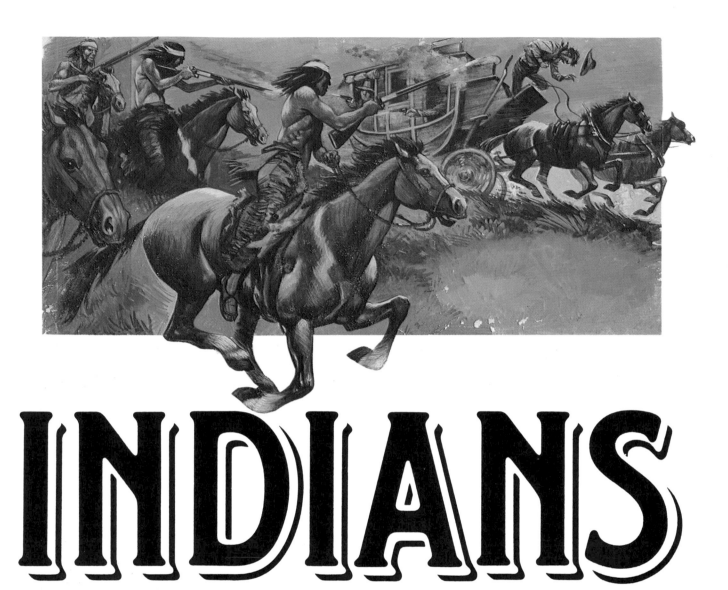

# INDIANS

It is a well-known fact that when Christopher Columbus first set foot on a little island in the year 1492, he believed he had reached India.

Columbus, though, was mistaken. He had not landed in India. He had arrived at an island that he named San Salvador. There is still argument as to which island it really was, but it is generally thought to have been one of the **Bahama Islands, north east of Cuba and south of Florida.**

Columbus mistakenly called the natives of this newly discovered continent Indians. For some reason, the name stuck. To this day, descendants of the people who were living in the Americas are usually referred to as Indians.

For almost 300 years after Columbus landed, the Indians fought the white invaders for the land that they rightfully believed was theirs. Not until December 1890 did they finally submit when 144 Sioux, men, women and children, died under the guns of their old enemy, the U.S. 7th Cavalry.

The story that follows relates some of the adventures of the most famous leaders of the Western tribes. They were all gallant men who were always prepared to lay down their lives for their just cause.

# WAR TO THE DEATH

To the first white men who came to America, the natives seemed to be living little better than stone age people. These European explorers saw only what the natives did not have; they did not notice or appreciate their rich culture.

At that time the Indians had no horses. There were no horses on the American continent. The Indians' utensils and weapons were made of grass, clay, wood, and stone. They fought and hunted with wooden bows and arrows and stone hatchets.

These natives were clever hunters, even though they had to hunt on foot. They knew the ways and habits of the animals they killed for food.

The arrival of the Europeans, particularly the conquistadores from Spain, must have shocked the simple Indians. These newcomers were greedy for gold and jewels, and the conquistadores were ruthless in their search for plunder. In no time they had turned the Indians into their enemies. Yet unknowingly the Spanish brought to the natives a great treasure: horses.

At first the natives thought that a mounted man and his horse were one animal. As soon as they understood that they were two separate beings and that horses could be mounted and used in the hunt, the Indians wanted them. They did their best to obtain as many as possible. They often bartered rich furs or gold nuggets for horses. Sometimes they just stole them instead.

Once they were mounted, the Plains Indians could hunt their favorite prey, the buffalo, more easily. The buffalo, also called the

**Horses were the Indians' dearest possessions. If they could not buy them, they would steal them.**

**The bison** (or buffalo as it is more generally known) **provided the Indians with food, clothes, ornaments and weapons.**

American bison, provided an Indian with all he needed: food, clothes, ornaments, and even some of his weapons. The Indians used every part of the buffalo in one way or another.

To the Plains Indians, buffalo was of vital importance. Should they be deprived of this animal, their way of life, and perhaps their very existence, was threatened. When white hunters started to kill off the great herds of buffalo, the Indians were outraged. Thousands of buffalo were killed to provide food for the Chinese and Irish workers who were laying railroad tracks across the country. The meat was eaten, but the remainder of the animal was wasted. The Indians saw this as a tragic loss.

In addition, thousands of settlers and ex-soldiers began pouring into the lands where they lived. To try to retain what was theirs, many Indian tribes took to the warpath. They were convinced that their only hope was to wipe out every white hunter, every white pioneer, and every paleface long-knife soldier who dared to enter their hunting grounds.

For the most part, it was war to the death between Indians and white invaders in the American West.

# RED CLOUD AND CRAZY HORSE STRIKE

*T*he U.S. Government often tried to adopt the appearance of fair dealing with the Indians. They drew up treaties in which they promised small sums of money to the Indians for Indian lands. If certain tribes were on the verge of attack, the government drew up treaties guaranteeing the Indians proper ownership of their territory. This was an admission on the part of the white government that the land did belong to the Indian people.

White people seldom kept their promises. Each time they broke treaties, they planted more bitterness in the hearts of the Indians who believed that the land belonged to God, to Manitou, the Great Spirit. No human had any more right to it than did the animals roaming the wide open spaces. The idea that land could be bought and sold was the white man's thinking. Indians entered into the treaties because they thought that this was the only way they could have peace.

Perhaps that was why Red Cloud, head war chief of the Sioux, agreed to a new treaty drawn up by the American Government. This treaty stated that the hunting grounds of the Sioux, Cheyennes, and Arapahos should remain their land forever and that no white settler should ever set foot on their territory.

This stretch of beautiful country lay between the Black Hills, the Rocky Mountains, and Yellowstone River. The Powder River ran through it, and the land was full of game.

The day came in 1866, however, when Red Cloud reined his sleek pony on the crest of a hill. He looked grimly down on the newly built army post of Fort Phil Kearny on the Bozeman Trail in what is today northern Wyoming. Red

**This photo was taken during an Indian delegation to Washington, D.C. The Indians (l. to r.) are Red Dog, Little Wound, Red Cloud, American Horse and Red Shirt. *(Photo: National Archives, Washington, D.C.)***

**Red Cloud, who was the head war chief of the Sioux Indians. *(Photo: National Archives, Washington, D.C.)***

Cloud's heart was full of hatred and bitterness, for once again the United States Government had broken its treaty. It had built a string of forts across the Indians' hunting grounds.

This time the Government's excuse was gold. Gold had been discovered in Idaho and Montana, and miners had at once headed for the gold fields.

By far the easiest and quickest route lay through the Indians' territory. The Government tried to make a new agreement with the Sioux and Cheyenne to build a road across their hunting grounds. The Indians refused. They knew that their lands would be overrun with land-grabbing white people. Within a short time, they would be driven out of their own territory.

With no regard for the Indians, the Government broke the treaty and ordered several forts to be built along the Bozeman Trail. These would protect the whites flocking to the gold fields.

In spite of many protests and warnings by the Indians, the forts were erected. Fort Phil Kearny was completed in the autumn of 1866.

While it was being built, Red Cloud and his warriors continually harassed the men, stealing horses, sniping and raiding supply wagons. They had done all they could to drive the soldiers away. When every effort failed, Red Cloud vowed to wage a full-scale war. He would attack the fort and destroy it.

As he gazed down on the army post, a majestic young warrior drew rein beside him. This was Crazy Horse, Red Cloud's fighting chief. He too, like Red Cloud, was an Oglala Sioux.

Indian chiefs were not as important as some novels and Hollywood films suggest. A brave was never obliged to fight. His "medicine" might be bad on a certain day. If he did not feel lucky, he would remain in his tepee. Thus a chief might set out on the warpath without a full muster of warriors. Nevertheless, Crazy Horse vowed to set a trap for the white pony soldiers the very next day.

The following morning was bitterly cold. The land was covered with a blanket of frost encrusted snow. It was December 21, 1866. A group of loggers left the fort and headed for the hillside to fell trees and saw logs. There were families in the fort, as well as officers and men, and much fuel was needed to keep the place warm. Suddenly a band of warriors swooped down on the wagons of the loggers.

On hearing shots, a young captain named William Fetterman swiftly led 80 cavalrymen out of the fort and raced to the assistance of the loggers. At once the Indians turned and fled. Fetterman galloped after them with his cavalrymen close behind. In doing so he disobeyed the orders of his commanding officer at the fort, Colonel Henry Carrington.

Carrington was wise in the cunning of the Indians. Fetterman, fresh from a brilliant career during the Civil War, was not. He led his men over a ridge in hot pursuit of the small band of Indians, straight into an ambush skillfully planned by Crazy Horse. Hundreds of Sioux, Cheyenne, and Arapaho warriors leaped from hiding places and let loose volleys of arrows with deadly accuracy.

Fetterman and his gallantly fighting soldiers were all dead after thirty minutes of hand-to-hand fighting. From that day forward the ridge on which they fought was known as Massacre Hill.

That night, a civilian scout, John "Portugee" Phillips, set out to ride 236 miles through blinding snow blizzards to Fort Laramie. He arrived there, completely exhausted, on Christmas night. He gasped out the news that Fort Kearny was being attacked by Indians. Two days later the relief force left Fort Laramie and headed for Fort Kearny.

In temperatures ranging between 25 and 45 degrees below zero, the relief force journeyed through raging snowstorms and drifts three feet deep. They finally reached Fort Kearny three weeks later.

After that the fort was under constant seige. Eight months later, Crazy Horse launched a fullscale attack on Fort Kearny. Nearly 2,000 painted warriors charged the fort. The soldiers, now armed with the latest breech-loading Springfield .55 caliber rifles, managed eventually to beat off the Indian assault.

Due to the bitter weather, Red Cloud and his warriors had not attempted another attack on the fort. They remained nearby, though, and were still determined to destroy it.

The fort remained under siege and continual harassment by Crazy Horse and his warriors for nearly a year. At last the garrison of Fort Kearny could stand the pressure no longer. The post was abandoned in August 1868.

Red Cloud and Crazy Horse watched the soldiers and their families leave. They were still in sight of the fort when Red Cloud gave the order to set the building on fire. Not until the fort was a smoldering mass of ashes and the last white soldier had disappeared from view, did Red Cloud and Crazy Horse wheel their ponies and ride away.

Red Cloud continued to be the leader and spokesman for the Oglala Teton Sioux and forsook the warpath. In November 1868 he signed a peace treaty with the U.S. Government. Two years later he was invited to Washington, where he had two meetings with President Ulysses S. Grant.

For the rest of his life, though, he hated the

**Crazy Horse vowed to Red Cloud that he would set a trap next day for the soldiers of Fort Kearny.**

white men. "They made us many promises," he said, "more than I can remember. They kept only one. They promised to take our land and they took it."

Red Cloud died in 1909 at the age of 87. As for Crazy Horse, he went on to lead the Oglala Sioux. They overwhelmed General George Armstrong Custer and his 264 troopers on the banks of the Little Big Horn River on June 25, 1876.

It was Crazy Horse of the Oglala Sioux who led the tribesmen who overwhelmed Custer and his troopers at the Battle of the Little Big Horn.

The following year, Crazy Horse with 2,000 warriors surrendered to the U.S. Cavalry. A few months later he was charged with causing more trouble. He attempted to escape and was killed by Private William Gentles, who stabbed the war chief with his bayonet. That night, September 5, 1877, Crazy Horse died. He was only 35 years old.

# THE WARPATH OF THE NEZ PERCE

*N*ot until 1863 did the Nez Perce, a peace-loving tribe of Indians, fight the white invaders of their land. They lived between the Blue Mountains in Oregon and the Bitter Root Mountains in Idaho.

They called themselves "The People." The name Nez Perce (pronounced nay per-say by the French but now commonly pronounced nezz purse) is French for "pierced noses." Only one small branch of the tribe actually pierced their noses. In 1835 this tribe came in contact with some French Canadian trappers who gave the name to the entire tribe.

When the white men came to their land, the Nez Perce welcomed them. They were open to new ideas, and greeted the missionaries and traders with open arms. The Nez Perce helped the white settlers to build a blacksmith shop and a saw mill. Many of them embraced the Christian religion. Three chiefs who had been converted signed a treaty with the United States at the great Walla-Walla Council of 1855. The Government treaty spelled out the boundaries of their territories. But it did not guarantee the Indians protection from land speculators and prospectors.

Trouble broke out when a prospector from California discovered gold in the Clearwater region of the Nez Perce hunting grounds. Miners began to pour into the territory.

**Chief Joseph of the Nez Perce Indians. (Photo: Bureau of American Ethnology).**

The Nez Perce were divided on the mining issue. Some chiefs wished to protect their lands and keep the miners out at all costs. Other chiefs were persuaded or bribed into allowing a certain amount of prospecting. It was a fatal move.

Gold fever brought thousands of speculators to the region. Tent towns sprang up overnight and soon steamboats were churning up the Columbia and Snake Rivers, laden with supplies for the miners. They swarmed all over the Nez Perce hunting grounds disregarding treaties and agreements.

# CHIEF JOSEPH'S FIGHTING RETREAT

In 1863 the Commissioners of Indian Affairs, acting under pressure from the various business companies that were now holding sway in the territory, called the Nez Perce chiefs to a council. They had drawn up a treaty that called for the removal of the Nez Perce to a reservation. Chief Joseph of the Wallowa Band of Lower Nez Perce refused to sign the treaty and warned all white men to stay away from his hunting grounds. The council broke up with no agreement.

Five years later a delegation of Nez Perce chiefs went to Washington to sign a treaty, on behalf of their people, agreeing to removal. All they wanted was a strip of land where they could live in peace.

Chief Joseph was not among them. He still stubbornly refused to give up the lands of his forefathers.

Other Nez Perce chiefs, among them Looking Glass and White Bird, also opposed the treaty and began to talk of war. Chief Joseph tried to restrain them, urging them to keep the peace no matter what the cost. "Better to live in peace than to begin a war and lie dead," he said. The pressures, however, were too great.

In June 1877, young Nez Perce warriors unable to contain their anger at their persecution any longer, painted themselves for war and raided along the Salmon River settlements, killing several pioneers. The countryside buzzed with news of the attack. Two companies of the First Cavalry, under Captain David Perry, were sent to protect the settlers. For the first time in their history, the Nez Perce were at war with the white men.

Chief Joseph had been so named by his white teacher, a missionary. His Indian name was Himmaton-Yalatkit, which means "Thunder Coming from the Water over the Land."

Joseph, now resigned to warfare, together with Chiefs Looking Glass, White Bird, and several warriors, waited for the cavalry in a canyon. The troopers rode straight into the ambush and were completely routed. Within minutes, the soldiers were riding for their lives

**The Nez Perce Indians had always lived at peace with the white people until gold was discovered in the Indians' hunting grounds.**

with a horde of screaming Indians hot on their heels.

Ten days later, the Indians learned that an army under the command of a one-armed U.S. General named Oliver Otis Howard was on the move. Joseph, Looking Glass, and White Bird soon discovered that their band of 300 warriors and their families were outnumbered ten to one. There was no hope now of saving their lands. The only course open to them was to cross the Bitter Root Mountains and escape to Canada.

Joseph did not like the idea of retreating. "What are we fighting for?" he asked. "Is it for our lives? No. It is for the land where the bones of fathers are buried. I do not want to die in a strange land. Remain with me here and we shall have plenty of fighting. Let us die on our own land."

He was outvoted. The Indians prepared to travel the long trail of 250 miles over the Bitter Root Mountains. The women and children gathered roots and berries for food. Rear and advance guards of warriors were on watch, and every man had a string of spare horses.

Then the fugitives set out, over winding ridges and along sudden precipices, through tangled undergrowth and pine forests. Some Indians were lost as they ventured across rock slides. Horses stumbled and fell as they tried to follow the tortuous paths.

The army anticipated the move Joseph made. General Howard followed the Nez Perce while another force moved in to block the Indians' path at the north end of the trail.

Joseph quietly eluded both forces and crossed the mountains safely into Montana. The weary travelers made camp on August 8 at the

Big Hole Basin. The next day they rested, but later that night they were attacked by a strong force of U.S. troopers under the command of Colonel John Gibbon. The Indians were taken completely by surprise but fought back valiantly. All night they battled hand-to-hand. The next morning the soldiers began to retreat, only to regroup and dig in. A great wail went up from the Indians' encampment. The ground was littered with the bodies of women and children who had died in the night attack. Among them was Chief Joseph's wife.

Army reinforcements were soon moving in the direction of the Big Hole Basin and once again the Nez Perce band turned north. Every turn they made was blocked by soldiers as the army bore down on the Indians. The ranks of the Nez Perce warriors were now thinning rapidly as they fought skirmish after skirmish with the soldiers.

Winter was closing in fast, and the Indians were exhausted by the months of pursuit and battle. The women and children suffered badly in the terrible cold. Fatigue and hunger weakened them still further. On and on through the snowswept Bear Paw Mountains they struggled. The old ones died by the wayside.

Only 30 miles from the Canadian border, a cavalry column under General Nelson Miles encircled the Nez Perce and attacked immediately. The Indians fought back, but during the fighting their horses were run off. Escape to Canada was made impossible.

General Miles had brought artillery with him, and now the big guns opened fire. The Indians fought on for another five days, firing from crude trenches, their wounded lying unattended. A raging blizzard enveloped them and added to their miseries.

On October 4, General Howard arrived with reinforcements, and for the Indians, all hope was gone. The next day, Chief Joseph surrendered. Only 87 warriors were still alive and half of these were wounded. He could not bear to see his people suffer any more. Handing his robe to General Miles he said: "I am tired of fighting. Our chiefs are killed. Looking Glass is dead. The old men are all dead. It is cold and we have no blankets. The little children are freezing to death. Hear me, I am tired. My heart is sick and sad. From where the sun now stands, I will fight no more forever."

Two years later the Nez Perce were herded onto a reservation in Oklahoma. Conditions were bad. There was no game to hunt, nor were there beautiful valleys and rich pastures for their horses. They were like babies, totally dependent on the Indian agent for their food. Exhaustion and sickness overtook them, and many died.

Joseph sent a petition to Washington, pleading for his people to be allowed to return to their lands. Then he added: "If I cannot go to my own home, let me have a home in some country where my people will not die so fast."

In May 1885 he and the Nez Perce survivors were allowed to return to the Northwest but not to Chief Joseph's beloved Wallowa Valley.

Joseph was a hero of the Indians and the white men alike. Yet still an exile from his lovely homeland, he died in 1904 on the Colville Reservation in Washington State.

# A COMANCHE NAMED PARKER

*I*n 1836, a thirteen-year-old white girl named Cynthia Ann Parker was kidnapped. A band of Comanche Indians took her during a raid on Parker's Fort on the banks of the Navasota River in Texas.

One of the most ruthless of the Comanche chiefs, Peta Nocona, later took Cynthia as his wife. They had two sons, Quanah and Pecos, and a daughter, Topasannah.

Fifteen years after her capture by the Comanches, Cynthia Ann was taken prisoner by a company of U.S. troopers and Texan settlers when they raided Peta Nocona's camp. At the time Peta Nocona and his warriors had gone

The Comanches raided forts and ranches throughout Kansas, Texas, Colorado, and New Mexico.

hunting. The raiders slew many Comanche women. They were about to kill Cynthia Ann when a Texas Ranger noticed her fair hair.

With her little daughter, Cynthia Ann was returned to her uncle, Isaac Parker, a rancher who had served with the U.S. Army. Her husband and two sons were not captured. They managed to escape into the boundless prairie.

Four years later, Cynthia's daughter died of a fever and the mother, stricken with grief, starved herself to death. Meanwhile Quanah Parker became a brilliant warrior under his chieftain father's guidance. When Peta Nocona died, Quanah became chief in his stead.

Quanah is a strange name for a fighting Comanche chief because it means "fragrant." The name was given to him by his mother, and Quanah refused steadfastly to change it. As Quanah Parker, he is renowed in the history of the Plains Indians of the old West. In 1871, when Quanah was 26 years old, Captain Ronald Mackenzie led a troop of U.S. cavalry on a special mission. He had been ordered to put an end to Comanche raids led by Quanah Parker.

If he hoped to surprise Quanah, he was mistaken. He and his men were bedded down for the night when, without warning, Quanah led his warriors in a headlong charge through Mackenzie's camp. The warriors fired into the air, stampeding the troopers' horses. Yelling with triumph, the Comanches rode off with as many horses as they could round up.

Ronald Mackenzie swore that one day he would have his revenge. His chance came three years later, in 1874. Several Comanches, Kiowas, and Cheyennes were camped in Palo Duro Canyon. Quite unexpectedly Mackenzie, now a colonel, happened to come upon them.

Quanah Parker had been leading his warriors through one territory after another — Kansas, Texas, Colorado, New Mexico. The Comanches enriched themselves at the expense of unsuspecting ranchers and settlers. They lost few men during their exploits and could congratulate themselves on the many horses and the amount of plunder that fell into their hands.

At last, the Government issued instructions to the Army that the Comanches were to be rounded up and forced to live on reservations. Troops poured into Comanche territory from all directions. Out of Fort Concho in Texas came Colonel Mackenzie, burning to avenge his defeat at the hands of Quanah Parker. Without delay he ordered his men to attack. His main aim was to drive off all the horses. Without them, the Comanches could be tracked down and captured without much difficulty. The attack was successful and the troopers drove off fourteen horses. Then while the infuriated Comanches watched helplessly, the soldiers drove the horses to a ridge above the Indian encampment and killed them all.

The soldiers had slain only a few Indians, but Quanah Parker knew that the days of the Comanche warpath were over. Elsewhere white soldiers captured one band of Comanches after another.

In 1875 Quanah led the survivors of his tribe to a reservation and surrendered. From then on he encouraged his people to follow the "white man's way." He did all he could to explain to them the importance of education and how much more comfortable it was to live in houses rather than in tepees. Perhaps his most difficult task was trying to persuade them to take up agriculture and forsake the warpath forever.

He was 66 years old when he died in 1911 near Fort Sill, Oklahoma. He and his mother today lie buried in the old military cemetery at Fort Sill.

# THE APACHE TERROR

Four hundred years ago, the Spanish conquistadores were riding northwards exploring California in search of gold and any other plunder. They also intended to establish missions and enslave the Indians. They came face to face with warriors who taught the cold-blooded Spaniards a lot about savagery, torture, and, above all, bravery against all odds.

The Spaniards called these ruthless tribesmen Coyoteros because they were as cunning as coyotes. The Zuni Indians though, called them Apache, meaning enemy. Enemies they were, as the other tribes already knew. The Spaniards and later white settlers paid a heavy price to discover this fact.

The United States began to take an interest in Arizona when huge balls of silver were found there in 1836. Prospectors flocked to the southwest. These miners soon found themselves enmeshed in a series of bitter wars with the Apaches.

In the 200 years since their first contact with the Europeans, the Apaches had adapted themselves well to the barren lands. Water and vegetation were scarce and few white men could survive in the landscape of volcanic rocks and blistering deserts.

Eight or more tribes were called by the general name of Apache. The most important were the Mescalero, Jicarilla, Mimbreños, Chiricahua, and Kiowa. The Chiricahua and several other tribes were grouped together and known as White Mountain Apaches.

No matter what their names, though, they were all pitiless, crafty, and distrustful. War was their business. They raided to obtain loot and slaves.

The young men of the tribe underwent a rigid initiation into the ranks of the warriors. They learned to stand and face the older braves who shot arrows at them. They had to dodge the arrows — or die.

When the sun was at its height, their mouths were filled with water and they were forced to run a course of many miles through difficult country. When they had finished their run, they had to spit out the water to show that they had not weakened and swallowed any.

They learned how to vanish like will o' the wisps in country that seemed to offer no cover and to strike where the enemy least expected them.

In the 1840s American settlers were pushing their way deeper into Arizona and New Mexico. Gold and silver strikes brought eager prospectors. To begin with the Apaches were not openly hostile. They hated the Spaniards and despised the Mexicans, but they approached the newcomers with curiosity.

One day, a group of miners, annoyed and suspicious of the Indians who persistently hung around their camp, seized one of them and tied him on the back of a wagon. They flogged him and drove him from their camp.

It was a recklessly stupid act, and the repercussions were terrifying. The man they had flogged was Mangus Colorado, a chief of the Mimbreños and related by marriage to chiefs of the Chiricahua and White Mountain bands.

For the rest of his life, Mangus Colorado made war. Mexicans, Spaniards, Americans — it mattered little. All the white men were his enemies.

The United States moved soldiers into the southwest and relations with the Apaches grew worse. White men hanged Apaches in retaliation for their raids. Apaches tortured white men to avenge the hangings.

In 1861, the Civil War broke out and the army garrisons in the southwest were recalled. At once the Apaches rampaged through the settlements, driving out the settlers and then destroying the homesteads.

Mangus Colorado and Cochise, chief of the Chricahuas, swept the territory clean and drove settlers into Tucson. Not long after even that town was reduced to a mere 200 inhabitants.

In 1862, General James H. Carleton marched from California with 3,000 volunteers to restore order in the Southwest. He launched a campaign of Apache extermination.

Miners and settlers were encouraged to return to Arizona and were offered rewards for Apache-killing expeditions. Bounty money was offered for Apache scalps.

Invitations to "talk peace" were sent out to the Apaches. Some, less distrustful than others, were shot down on arrival. Even Mangus Colorado was half-convinced by the offer of peace treaties. He was now an old man, and perhaps he believed that the "white-eyes" would treat him with kindness, especially if he rode in completely alone. If this is so, he made a big mistake.

Old he might have been, but he was a big man, proud and unafraid. He made the "long-knife" soldiers look like pigmies as they surrounded him, with faces scowling and rifles cocked.

During the night, as the soldiers and the

Apaches were pitiless, crafty and distrustful, who fought the white men fearlessly.

Apache chief lay beside a campfire, the troopers heated their bayonets in the fire. They thrust the hot steel at Mangus Colorado's feet. When the chief at last protested, they shot him dead. The official report on the death of Mangus Colorado was that he had died while "trying to escape."

In spite of his ferocious campaign, General Carleton failed to conquer the Apaches. They were pushed further and further into their inaccessible mountain hideouts and driven to still greater acts of merciless savagery.

The war dragged on. By 1871, it had cost the United States Government $40 million and 1,000 lives. It had accomplished nothing.

In February 1871, 150 members of the tribe of Arivaipa Apaches, came into Fort Grant. Their leader, Eskiminzin, said that his people were tired. Weary of the continual warfare, they now wanted to live in peace. They were given a strip of land near Tucson.

Two months later, on April 18, a mob of settlers marched out of Tucson and sprang a surprise attack on the Apaches. One hundred and eight men and women were slain and 29 children taken and sold into slavery.

The massacre caused a national outcry. One hundred men who had taken part in the slaughter were arrested and tried. They were declared not guilty by the jury.

A worried government sent General George Crook to Arizona. He was an expert Indian fighter but also a humane man. He was sympathetic towards the Indians, and his policy was one of understanding and peace. By 1874, all the important tribes had been won over or rounded up. The Apaches forsook the warpath and settled on the reservations.

**Various bands of Apaches ran wild along the border country.**

# GERONIMO REBELS

The Apaches tried to settle down to agency life. They planted crops, only to see them fail in the barren soil.

Many white agents swindled the Apaches out of supplies and made money illegally by selling reservation lands. The women and children grew hungry. The warriors drifted into apathy and drunkeness. Once proud warriors were made to wear metal tags like dogs. One by one the various bands left the reservations and ran wild along the border country.

It is now that the notorious chief Geronimo enters our story. He was a medicine man and chief of the Chiricahua Apaches. His Apache name was Goyathlay, which means "One Who Yawns." The Mexicans called him Geronimo.

In 1876 when he was 42, he led a runaway band into Mexico. The United States Government had ordered all Apaches onto the San Carlos Agency in Arizona. Some time later, Geronimo and his followers were rounded up and also taken to San Carlos. They settled for a time, but were always discontented.

Geronimo's answer was to take to the war-path again. Once more the army was sent out after him, and he was forced to surrender. Not

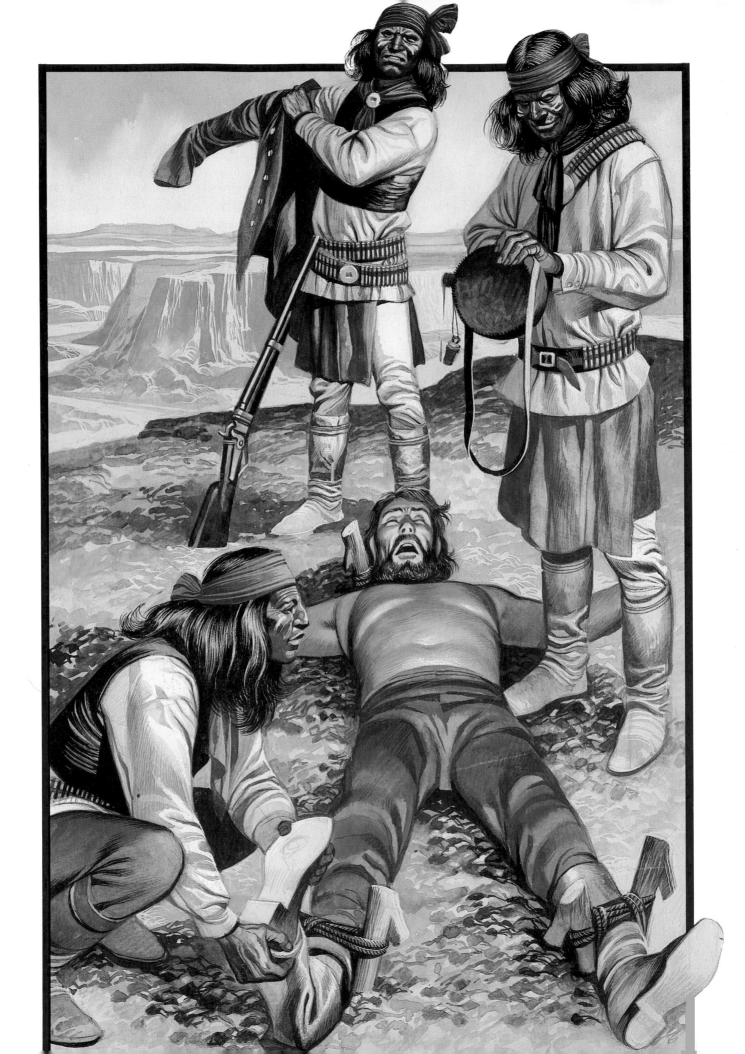

for long, though, did he live a peaceful life. The U.S. Government again forced him to forsake the ways of peace.

The Apaches liked drinking tiswin, a liquor which the Chiricahuas brewed from corn. The U.S. Government tried to ban the drink, because the Apaches became drunk and very troublesome when they drank tiswin.

Banning tiswin was enough reason for Geronimo to gather together a band of renegade Indians and once more ride the war trail. They raided white settlements in Arizona and Mexico and killed settlers. Any white men that fell into the hands of the Apaches were often tortured. Staking their victims out in the burning Arizona sun was a favorite Apache method of torture. General George A. Crook, a veteran Indian fighter, was ordered to capture or kill Geronimo and his warriors.

In March 1886, Geronimo and Crook met and arranged a treaty. Once more Geronimo broke away and headed for the border.

General Nelson A. Miles was dispatched to capture Geronimo. He formed the Apache Scouts and put Lt. Charles B. Gatewood in charge. Gatewood found out the location of Geronimo's camp and went in unarmed. He spent two days talking to Geronimo. In August 1886, Geronimo surrendered for the last time. He and 340 of his followers were taken to Florida. The old warrior was enslaved at hard labor for four years. He and his Chiricahuas were brought west again and settled in Fort Sill in Oklahoma.

He became a Christian and died a prisoner of war at Fort Sill in 1909. He was about 75. Geronimo was the last of the Apache war chiefs.

*Above:* **Geronimo, merciless enemy of the white men. (Photo: The Bettmann Archive).**

*Left:* **The Apaches would stake out their prisoners in the burning Arizona sun).**

# THE FIGHTING CHEYENNES

*L*ike the Nez Perce Indians, the Cheyennes were at first friendly toward the white people. In 1851, they attended the Great Council at Fort Laramie. There 10,000 Plains Indians signed an agreement with the U.S. Government and agreed to accept the territorial boundaries laid down in the treaties.

Once again the treaties were broken. As in the case of the Nez Perce, the discovery of gold and the resulting flood of miners caused the Cheyennes to take to the warpath.

Black Kettle, a chief of the Cheyennes, tried hard to preserve peace. He brought his people into Sand Creek, 40 miles northeast of Fort Lyon, Colorado. He even flew the Stars and Stripes over his tepee to show his loyalty.

At dawn on November 29, 1864, a band of Colorado Volunteers under the command of Colonel John M. Chivington, attacked the Cheyenne camp.

Many reasons have been given for this unprovoked attack. The Colorado miners hated the Cheyennes. But some people feel that it was a deliberate attempt to start an Indian war. The Colorado Volunteers would then have a reason to remain where they were and would not be drawn into the Civil War that was then raging in the East.

Whatever the reason, the attack was a cold-blooded massacre. It was condemned by the entire nation. Cheyenne men, women, and children were ruthlessly shot down and killed. Black Kettle managed to escape, and the entire frontier erupted in warfare.

Custer led his 7th Cavalry into Black Kettle's village and slew more than 100 Cheyenne warriors.

Apaches, Kiowas, Comanches, Sioux, and Cheyennes took to the warpath. Colorado Territory was cut off from communication with the East. A campaign under General Winfield Scott Hancock failed to defeat the Indians. In 1868, General George Armstrong Custer took to the field with the 7th Cavalry.

In November 1868, Black Kettle and his followers were camped along the frozen Washita River. It was a hard winter and snow lay inches thick across the prairie. As the sky began to lighten, the still air was shattered by the sound of bugles, and Custer's 7th Cavalry came charging into the village. The Indians were taken completely by surprise. Black Kettle and more than a hundred of his warriors were slain.

For the next 10 years, the U.S. Army fought to subdue the Plains tribes. The Indian stood in the path of white man's progress. There was no longer room for him anywhere.

In 1865, the construction gangs of the Union Pacific and Kansas Pacific Rail roads began to inch their way across the Great Plains. Thousands of Irish immigrants set out to lay a mile of track each working day, and the steel rails began to eat into the prairies. The Iron Horse was sounding the death knell for the Cheyennes.

In 1870, leather factories in the East were offering high prices for buffalo hides. So buffalo hunters, including Buffalo Bill Cody, descended upon the herds and began to slaughter them in their thousands.

The buffalo was the mainstay of the Indians. Their lives depended on it. In one fateful decade millions of animals were cut down to a mere handful. Cheyenne warriors joined other Indians in derailing the trains and attacking the hunters. Now, they were fighting for survival against hopeless odds.

Then in 1876, the Cheyennes and the Sioux, whose chief medicine man was Sitting Bull, struck back with a vengeance. On June 25, hundreds of Indian warriors led by Crazy Horse drove Custer and his men up a slope of the Little Big Horn and slew them. Custer had paid in full for his pitiless attack on Black Kettle's camp eight years earlier.

A year later the Cheyennes agreed to surrender to the U.S. Army. General Crook held a council with the Cheyennes, and they agreed

George Armstrong Custer, doomed to die with his men at the Battle of the Little Big Horn. (Photo: National Archives, Washington, D.C.)

to give up their lands and move to a reservation in Oklahoma.

The new territory was far from their own hunting grounds. There were no buffalo, and game of any description was scarce. The Indians had to depend on the Indian agency to supply Texas cattle for food. Sickness overtook the Cheyennes, and they began to yearn for their own lands and their old way of life.

In July 1878, more than 300 Cheyennes left the reservation to "go home." The men,

women, and children were under the leadership of a chief named Dull Knife.

For six months the little band outwitted the thousands of soldiers sent to bring them in. Through blizzards and storms they struggled against overwhelming odds to reach their old hunting grounds.

On January 18, 1879, less than half of them reached the Platte River. There they surrendered to Lieutenant William P. Clark. General Crook petitioned the U.S. Government on their behalf, and they were given a reservation on the Tongue River and allowed to stay. There their descendants still live proudly as the Northern Cheyenne. They maintain close contact with others of their tribe in Oklahoma, the equally proud Southern Cheyenne.

In the days of their glory, no Indians were more respected by the white people than the "Fighting Cheyennes."

# THE END OF THE WAR TRAIL

Sitting Bull, medicine man of the Hunkpapa Sioux. *(Photo: Smithsonian Institution, National Anthropological Archives, Washington, D.C.)*

**R**ed Cloud and Crazy Horse were two very well-known Sioux chiefs. Equally well-known was a third chief. He was Sitting Bull, the medicine man and tribal chief of the Hunkpapa Sioux.

When he was 10 years old, he rode out on his first buffalo hunt. He was only 14 when he fought bravely in a skirmish with some Crow Indians. He was then known as Jumping Badger, but after his first fight he took the name of Four Horns.

For some reason he was not content with this name either. When he was 23 years of age, he became a medicine man and adopted the name of Sitting Buffalo Bull.

Sitting Bull was always involved with Sioux affairs. During the next 12 years, he became very important both as a warrior and adviser. At powwows his words were always listened to by the fighting chiefs.

His, fame today, probably stems from his presence at the Battle of the Big Horn, Custer's Last Stand. On the day General Custer and his men were killed on the banks of the Little Big Horn River by a combined army of Sioux and Cheyennes, Sitting Bull was the Indian leader.

Although Sioux chiefs Crazy Horse and Gall were prominent during the battle, Sitting Bull was not. Later, it was said that he was off somewhere "making medicine." No one doubts, though, that Sitting Bull was a very brave Indian.

After the battle, Sitting Bull headed for the Canadian border with a large band of Sioux. There he believed he would be safe from the vengeance of pursuing U.S. cavalry.

He stayed in Canada for five years and then returned to the United States and surrendered. In 1885, he appeared in person with Buffalo Bill Cody in Cody's Wild West Show. People flocked to see the man who had defeated the great General Custer. When he rode into the arena during the performances, he was loudly hissed by audiences.

The medicine man, as it turned out, had not yet finished causing the white people trouble.

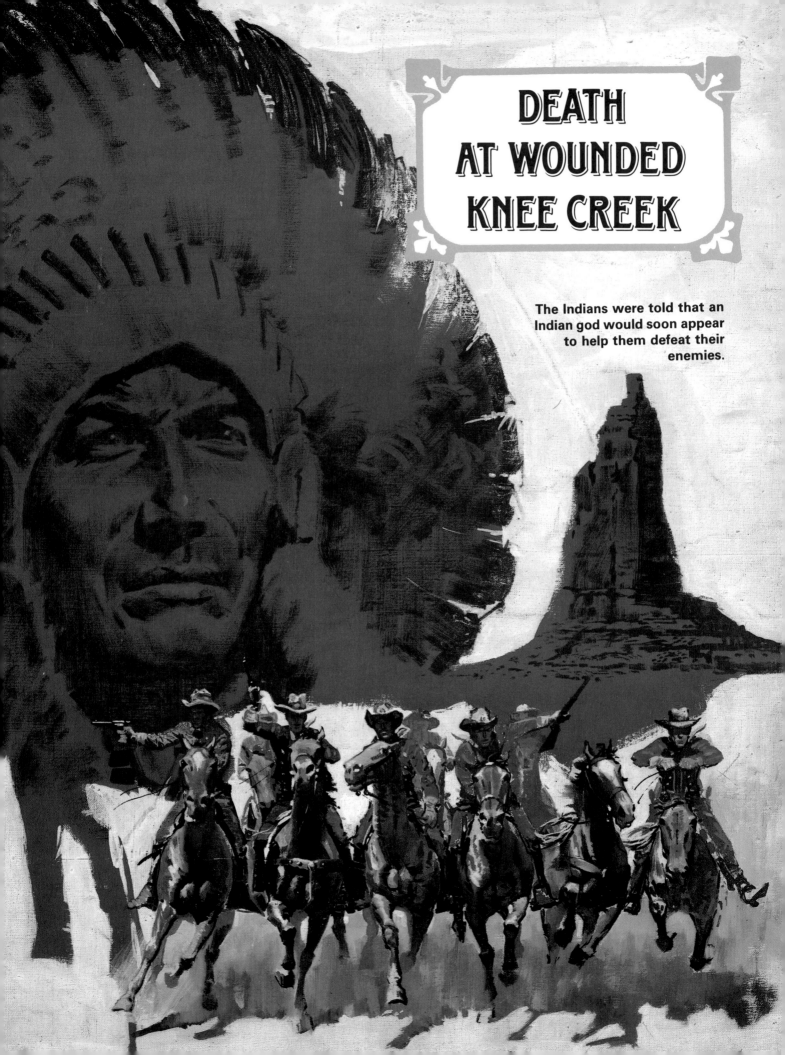

# DEATH AT WOUNDED KNEE CREEK

The Indians were told that an Indian god would soon appear to help them defeat their enemies.

*I*n 1888, a young Piute Indian named Wovoka fell ill with a fever and had a dream. He said that the "Great Spirit" came to him and told him that an Indian god would soon appear. This god would return all the stolen lands to the Indians. All their dead friends would be brought back to life. The living Indians had only to sing and dance and pray. While the news spread among the super-stitious Indians, an eclipse of the sun took place. They took this as a sign that Wovoka's prophecy was to be believed. Several other Indians fell into trances, all claiming that a great Indian triumph was on its way.

Sitting Bull now stepped forward to support this belief. In 1890, Indians across the West were dancing the Ghost Dance and wearing Ghost Dance shirts. These were decorated with magic symbols and the Indians thought they were bullet-proof.

The U.S. Government became alarmed by the unrest and ordered the capture of Sitting Bull. When they arrived at his cabin, agency officers found it surrounded by hostile sup-porters, who tried to prevent his arrest. In the fight that followed, Sitting Bull and one of the agency policemen were killed. The desperate resistance put up by the Indians of North America to retain ownership of their lands was now drawing rapidly to a close.

Angry Sioux began to assemble, and most of them truly believed that no harm could befall them as long as they wore their Ghost Dance shirts. Army detachments were sent out to put an end to the menace. Among them was the 7th Cavalry, Custer's old regiment.

The Indians were called upon to surrender, and many of them did. There was one band led by Chief Big Foot of the Minneconjou Sioux. He was old and suffering from pneumonia, but even so he ordered his followers to make for the Pine Ridge Agency, there to lay down their arms. Before they could reach the agency, the Sioux were overtaken by troopers of the 7th Cavalry under the command of Colonel James W. Forsyth.

The date was December 29, 1890, in the middle of winter. The ground was covered with snow and the weather was bitterly cold.

**A ghost-shirt. The Indians believed that such shirts would protect them from the guns of the U.S. troopers. (Photo: Bureau of American Ethnology.)**

The cavalry, reinforced with four Hotchkiss cannons, surrounded Big Foot's camp. Forsyth called upon the Indians to surrender their arms. Only two guns were produced. This enraged the colonel, and he ordered his sol-diers to search the camp. When the Sioux pro-tested, the soldiers began to knock down the tepees and push around the women and children. Reports differ as to what happened next, but it appears that an Indian shot a trooper. Instantly the Indians were mown down. When the fighting ended scarcely an Indian was still alive.

Sioux warriors, their old people, their women, their children, even their ponies, were gunned down in an orgy of slaughter. Some accounts stated that as many as 300 were shot down, while others reported that some 150 died. Of the troopers, about eight were killed. It is believed that several of these were slain accidentally by their comrades during the indiscriminate shooting.

This was the "battle" of Wounded Knee. Indian warriors in their pride would never again ride the war trail. Their gallant but futile effort to keep their hunting grounds was over.

# TRIBES AND CUSTOMS

Apaches, Cheyennes, Sioux, Comanches, and Nez Perce were not the only tribes who fought to retain their hunting grounds. Others, too, are famous in Western history. Among them are the Blackfeet, the Crows, the Navajos, the Arapahos, the Shoshones, the Pawnees, and the Utes, after whom the state of Utah was named.

The many Indian tribes of North America rarely spoke the same language. Some tribes, such as the Sioux (their correct name is Dakota), were made up of a number of smaller tribes. For example, there were the Two Kettles, Sissetons, Oglalas, Tetons, Hunkpapas, Brulés, Santees, Yanktons, Minneconjous, Assiniboins, Midewakantons, and Sans Arcs. Their languages were similar. They dressed differently from other major tribes.

In truth, it would be impossible to state how many different tribes there were in America before the white man came. Many tribes have now died out. J. Fenimore Cooper's famous classic, *The Last of the Mohicans*, describes one such case.

The names of the tribes were often descriptive. Blackfeet were called that for one of two possible reasons. The first was that members of the tribe wore black moccasins. The other reason is that an enemy tribe had once carried out a raid, taken all their horses, and set fire to the prairie. When the Blackfeet trudged through the smoke-blackened grass, it stained their moccasins. The Dakotas, the large tribe with many sub-tribes, means "allies." For many years the Hunkpapa Sioux had the right to camp at the head of any Sioux gathering. Hunkpapa means "Those Who Camp At The Entrance."

Different names, different clothes, and different languages were abundant. In one way, however, Indians all over North America won the reluctant admiration of the white people. They were, with very few exceptions, extremely brave. They were ready to die for their families, their homes, and their way of life.

The Plains Indians were often on the move because they depended on the buffalos. As buffalo herds moved across the prairies in search

of grass to eat, the Indians followed the herds.

Buffalo meat was cut into strips and then dried in the sun. Preserved in that way for a long time, the meat was eaten during the winter when food was difficult to find.

Moccasins, clothes, bedding, shields, tepees, and snowshoes were all made out of buffalo hides. Sinews were used as thread for sewing and also for bowstrings. Their domestic utensils, such as drinking cups and spoons, were fashioned out of the animals' bones. Glue was made out of buffalo hooves. It is easy to understand, therefore, why the wholesale slaughter of the herds by white hunters, who took only the meat to eat, drove so many Indians to the warpath.

The evening before Indians rode out to attack, they would gather for the war dance. Each warrior would dance around in a circle and sing. He would appeal to his own "medicine" for protection against harm and evil spirits. This "medicine" could be a sacred object or a good luck amulet. It might even be a tree. All hoped that the religious rites, that were carried out during the war dance, would ensure the defeat of their enemies.

The Indian prized his horse above all his other possessions. Without it, he could not hunt buffalo and he could not ride out to war. Horses were always tethered close to tepees at nightfall and guarded by sentries. During the night, a raid might be launched for the sole purpose of stealing a tribe's horses. Any captured horse thief would be put to death.

Until the coming of the white man, the Indians had never thought of the wheel. They used a litter when transporting their possessions from one camp to another. This litter was called a travois. Until the Spaniards brought horses to America, the travois was pulled by hand or by a dog.

Today many of the Indians' traditions and ways of life have disappeared. Busy highways and railroads now cross the prairies where the buffalo roamed and the Indian hunted. Ranchlands, fertile fields and farms dot the plains. The traditional life patterns of the Indians will never return in full.

Today, many tribes are working to regain their cultural heritage. Young children are taught the dances and arts of the old days. Indians on reservations are forming their own businesses and marketing to non-Indians. The land belonging to a reservation is recognized as a separate nation, regulated by its own laws. Some reservations even issue their own license plates.

No longer is the culture of Native Americans measured by European standards. Little by little, non-Indians are coming to appreciate and admire the art of American Indian tribes for its beauty and craftsmanship. So, too, is there a newfound admiration for the traditional way of Indian life, which took only what it needed from nature to survive.

**He Dog, one of Crazy Horse's warriors. An Amulet, probably for good luck, hangs from his neck.**

# IN THE DAYS OF THE INDIANS

| | |
|---|---|
| 1680-1692 | The Pueblo Indians of the Southwest revolt against the Spanish rule. |
| 1689-1763 | The French and Indian Wars are fought between France and Britain for possession of North America. |
| 1784 | The Iroquois Indians of New York are forced to cede all their lands west of the Niagara River. |
| 1800 | The Cherokee Indians of the mid-Atlantic states adopt some ways of the whites. They begin plantations and own slaves. They establish a Republican form of government called the Cherokee nation. |
| 1821 | Sequoya, a Cherokee Indian, invents a system of writing for the Cherokee language. |
| 1824 | Fur trappers enter the Northwest Territory to hunt, and disagreements arise with the local Indians. |
| 1830 | Congress passes the Indian Removal Act forcing all Indians living east of the Mississippi River to give up their lands and move west. |
| 1837 | Osceola, chief of the Seminole tribe in Florida, is captured. The Seminole Wars end with the tribe nearly wiped out. |
| 1838-1839 | The Cherokee Indians begin their long journey on foot to the Oklahoma Territory. Many die along the way. The forced march is known as the "Trail of Tears." |
| 1861 | The Civil War begins over the issue of slavery. |
| 1861-1900 | The Apache Wars begin during the Civil War. Cochise and Geronimo are two chiefs who lead raids on outposts in the southwest. |
| 1865 | President Lincoln is assassinated and the Civil War ends. |
| 1866 | Indians are forced to cede half of Oklahoma to white settlers. |
| 1874 | Gold is discovered in the Black Hills of South Dakota. Fighting breaks out between the Sioux and whites looking for gold. |
| 1876 | General George Armstrong Custer and over two hundred men are wiped out by the Sioux in retaliation for the Sioux defeat at Little Big Horn, Montana. It is called "Custer's Last Stand." |
| 1889 | The Sioux are forced to cede 9,000,000 acres to the government. |
| 1890 | The Dakota Sioux stage the "Ghost Dance War." |
| 1890 | The Sioux Wars end. Great chiefs like Sitting Bull and Crazy Horse are either dead or captured. |
| 1890 | Oklahoma is organized as a territory. |
| 1894 | The end of the Red River War between the army and the Arapaho and Cheyenne of the Southern Plains. |